The Canary's Songbook

KAREN PRESS was born in Cape Town, South Africa. She has worked as a teacher of mathematics and English, and with a range of independent projects developing models of progressive education. She has published seven collections of poetry and has also written textbooks and other education materials in the fields of mathematics, science, economics and English, as well as children's stories, a film script and stories for newly literate adults. In 1987 she co-founded the publishing collective Buchu Books. She currently works as a freelance editor and writer, and is an associate of the national advice and information support service for South African writers, The Writers' Network, which she helped to establish.

T0159866

Also by Karen Press from Carcanet
Home

KAREN PRESS

The Canary's Songbook

CARCANET

Acknowledgements

For offering me tranquil space in which to work on the poems in this collection, I am grateful to Anne von der Heiden and Hans-Hagen Hildebrandt in Sompriezzo, Max and Delayne Loppert in Refrontolo, Carola Luther in Sowerby Bridge and Brendan and Ann Butler in Edinburgh. I thank the Rockefeller Foundation for the residency they granted me at the Bellagio Study and Conference Centre in 2002, during which a substantial part of the preparation of the collection was undertaken.

Versions of some of the poems in this volume first appeared in *Carapace*, *New Coin*, *PN Review* and on the website www.poetryinternational.org.

First published in Great Britain in 2005 by
Carcanet Press Limited
Alliance House
Cross Street
Manchester M2 7AQ

A CIP catalogue record for this book is available from the British Library
ISBN 1 85754 763 2

The publisher acknowledges financial assistance from Arts Council England

Typeset by XL Publishing Services, Tiverton
Printed and bound in England by SRP Ltd, Exeter

Contents

The sea roaring softly

The sea roaring softly
and a plane flying over it
roaring into the distance.

The tide so far out
the rock pools become rolling hills,
brown grass and green grass, curling.

Springtime of the world
when the sun shone
gently on shallow water.

Softly something crashes
far away, like a child's cough
when its mother is near.

I

Broken bits of the past

Broken bits of the past
find their way into my pockets

bright as the eyes of stray dogs,
pleading and fierce.

In sympathy the present hammers itself to pieces
and climbs in there.

Cement – we need cement now,
wood glue, paper glue, fixatives, bonding agents,

they should issue all schoolchildren with enough,
send them back to the land

to cement it in place, cement down their parents,
make plaster casts of bones to bury there as ancestors,

order indigenous trees from catalogues
and plant them everywhere to stabilise the sand,

bury the smashed masks and pots
deep in the ground to keep it drained,

feed the dogs and send them on their way,
settle things, settle them down once and for all.

Knocking series

1   So you begin

So you begin by arriving
at a front door.

You hear a sound like water falling,
but the walls of the house are dry.

Knock, or listen carefully
standing to one side, in shadow.

Will you be recognised?
Is your name known here?

You must knock, the only way out
is through this door.

The forest is all around you
and if your house is here

then surely it is the forest where you live?
Surely your shadow will know its way

among the old low swaying branches,
among the fresh leaves and broken twigs

pointing backwards and forwards?

2 Walls of wisteria

Walls of wisteria waylay me everywhere.
I'm trying to find my way to the wild place
where drums summon the dead to speak
but the wisteria captures me in sweetness
and I can't pass through.

I tear at the blossoms, looking for thorn trees locked in dry earth.
Beyond the soft clusters are hedges of rosebuds,
beyond them the olive and almond trees amble,
beyond them the boundary of cypresses stands guard
implacably peaceful.

I light fires in the meadow with the songs of tall desert women,
but the wisteria lays its lilac light over my skin,
the cypresses send a mist of songbirds through my hair,
the roses bring my mother and father to me in dreams
so that I'll stay here.

3 Taller than my shadow

When I go home to honour my ancestors
they gather round me like hitchhikers
clamouring to join me on my travels.

I say to them what is the best way?
And they always answer:
you will show us.

Year by year I grow taller
and the bag on my back grows heavier
with wriggling ghosts.

At night the ancestors pay their way
by sending me dreams.
I wake having been in so many former living rooms

I have no idea how to redecorate my house
or what to do with the garden,
and several letters of apology seem necessary.

That house

The green light of those rooms,
the walls that ignored us,
the strange preoccupied silence in doorways.
We weren't the ones expected.

The photographs filling the walls of the breakfast room.
I thought of cold toast, a butler serving kidneys.
People we were in some sense descended from.
Our mother's face not there, nor her mother's.

We could go in and out of bedrooms,
run up and down the long passages,
bang on the black piano's brown keys.
The house gave no sign of hearing us.

In the back room an old woman had retreated
into a world of paper bags and string.
She gave us plastic windmills and rewarded our mother with dried fruit
for having loved her when young.

When you're older you'll understand

Strangers lay claim to me
in the house of the dead.

I sleep with their hands around my throat.
My father tries to protect me.

They abandoned my mother.
She dresses me to please them.

Séance

Is anybody there?
Hold hands, don't break the circle.
Is anybody there?

Who else is out there?
The ones who talk always have nothing to say
that couldn't be written on a postcard: tell Lionel not to worry,
I send my love, Dorothy says she's watching over you.
Or was that Dora?

You wonder what deals are being struck on the other side,
who's paying whom to send a reassuring word,
to swallow back old hatreds.
Do they gather eagerly at a doorway, waiting to be summoned?
Is there bitter disappointment there too,
a need for consolation afterwards,
are séances held by the dead to call up the living?

The hands around the table grow hot and cold without reason.
The glass jerks between letters like a slow literacy student.
Where are the ones who know more than we do,
the ones dancing through firelit trees among sleeping birds?

Turn on the light.
We'll have tea in the Rosenthal cups and saucers,
the ones your grandmother left you.
Here we all are, after all.
Those cups are fragile, don't hold them too fiercely.

Shrines

A photograph.
On one side two sticks of incense in a tray of sand.
On the other side a flower in a cup.
Four pebbles. A bowl with water. A candle.
The cloth beneath it all is dark red or black.
The wall behind it all is covered in the same cloth.
It is a narrow shelf or table, at eye level for a kneeling person.

I kneel here every day, adjust things, light the candle, practise
for the time when I've forgotten that the layout of this shrine
comes from a photograph in *National Geographic*,
and something may begin to happen here that changes me –
the photograph to speak,
a door to open in the covered wall.

Treasure trail

How did you know?
I find them now

as I need them:
the Neruda volume,

the Zen anthology,
the Horowitz recordings.

You laid a trail quietly
and left, left your warm gown,

left the incense wrapped in thin paper,
the matches in your pocket, still dry.

I remember the saxophone you sold
before I was born.

When I hear it now
I know I'm walking in the right direction.

I look up and see you on the horizon,
walking along it, looking for something.

Stones for my pockets

Burying our mothers one by one
we float away,

the good girls and the bad girls.
No one will ever ask again,

when are you coming home?
All the suitcases empty themselves and leave us.

After the first freefall hours of grief
we'll become sirens or sibyls, ageless, untouchable.

One friend captures her mother's hands again and again
on cloth, glass, paper.
One pins down with words a certain neatness of the eyes,
a certain folded pain.
One spins her babies into swirls of paint petals
in their grandmother's autumn.

I collect your stories,
stones for my pockets
to hold me down
when the root goes.

The poem each woman poet writes

There is a woman who does not phone
unless she is sure she won't disturb,
who leans as lightly as a photograph on my arm,
who asks nothing now, having taken everything
I had to give her without ever saying
'This is not enough'. And she can't be blamed
if I lie in the night imagining her
lying in the night wondering what happened,
what else she could have done
to give birth to me differently.

Men wear the secret masks

Men wear the secret masks
and blow the flutes.
These are the voices of ancestral birds
singing of their warrior deeds.

The women must never see
the men blowing their flutes.
If a woman sees the bird
become a man, he kills her.

This happens in every house.
There is always an ancestral bird
in the shape of a man
singing in the shape of a flute.

There is always a woman
seeing something that could kill her.

Living children and dead children

1

When I think of living children I think of them walking
small and alone over wide hard ground
strewn with curling thorns the colour of scorpions
and leaves as strong as shoes, as strong as skin.
I think of them walking with straight backs
in the direction of hills far away,
and the low trees watching them in case they need help,
and the grasshoppers following them
to find out where they're going,
and an eagle circling that doesn't dare to swoop.

There is no magic garden there, and no giant to learn to trust.

I think of them as ones who never turn back or cry
because everyone is so far away
and the land is wide open even in darkness,
the stones stay warm as loaves of bread,
the night moths hover,
fly forward a little way,
hover and watch.

2

Dead children are no one's ancestors.
They sit alone, unsummoned,
and all their memories surround them.

No one comes to fold the memories away,
wash their faces, sing them to sleep.
Their knowledge takes the form of hunger.

Around them their successor dead,
parents and grown siblings, nieces, nephews,
bustle about, preparing for ceremonies of power over the living.

The dead children, ancestors of death,
sit on the floor between the swirling hems of shadows,
lost.

II

In Jakob's house

1

On one morning, Jakob, holding my hand
though I was holding yours, you took me
from my first apple and honey breakfast
among Rodchenko's functional dreams,
through the heroin-haunted station
into your most recent city.

We wandered between galleries of life-size traps
for animals and people built of recycled materials,
down a long dinner table of sculpted silent men,
through open-legged streets of Japanese whore-children
pinned to the walls and out into the mediaeval square
where roasted almonds, gingerbread and spiced wine
played their flutes around your voice
leading me further than I had come.

Pierced by the winter sun's bleak eyes we sat
bare-headed drinking coffee after coffee,
watching the exiled Roma women
perform their desperation for us.

Inside your unfolding story of the century's failure
you ushered me past the monumental mechanical worker
striking the air over the heads of Frankfurt's electronic princes,
through scaffold towers and across pavements drilled open
to receive new steel roots, into the darkness
of the tiny shop where chocolates are made
according to a treasured recipe, and chose
ten small perfections for your anxious beloved.

Jakob, how many worlds have you survived?
I know you only in swallow swoops inside a few journeys,
drinking briefly from the small bowls you leave
in places I might pause to sip.

You've read everything and you're out walking to work
in your eighty-sixth year, in this century full of dying struggles
you step sure-footed into the next skyscraper shadow
convinced that human beings are still growing towards the sun.

Were you always this whole-hearted?
Did you stand on a silent threshold one year
looking at your bombed past and grow
thinner than unfed dogs in the frozen street?

You are the century that rescued Europe from itself,
the man who still carries Kristallnacht's splinters in his pocket,
who's read the bankers' ransom notes to governments
and the eyes of women with drugged babies
invading suburban trains, Kandinsky's colours
and Bill Viola's roaring brain music,
and who draws his comrades of all countries
into the late November wind
to review their mistakes and plan their next campaign.

Leaving again for my southern home
I think about the first journey of a family
that did not have the strength to carry you
inside its memories, inside its hopes.
May I choose you now, Jakob, as my father's father,
the one he never knew? Is it too late?

2

In Jakob's house I feel welcome.
And it is Sigi's house and it is she who welcomes me
inside her diamond-cutter's gaze,
letting Jakob's story fill the air like incense,
her own smoke curling privately along the walls.
She's chosen this, it suits her
to be left out of the light
that washes what she's seen away from itself.

Sometimes she brings a quiet set of inverted commas
out of her smile to place around him.
Often she shakes her head as he talks.
Her life is full of the history
he hopes will lead to better things.

Through my guest room walls
their voices come during the night,
tumbling embrace of Schumann's cadences,
braced spine of Brecht's chords.

3

Dear Jakob, where I come from there are men like you
but their memories are shorter. They read no poetry
because the distances are too great between hunger and a plan.
Wide-eyed with commitment, stopping nowhere long enough.

Where I live time is so new that those in power
wear gold-plated watches bigger than their hearts.
Your continent's horrors were my childhood fables.
Mine come roaring at me in three dimensions of sunlit misery
louder than my language. Here love is never
the answer to anyone's weeping

and I hunger so for that landscape of intimate struggles,
willingness to save one person at a time.
Easily seduced by darkness stories
offered like bitter chocolate in a bright room,
my longings twine around the wrought-iron ruins of lives
fire-bombed into a lacework of suffering,
wrapped in old furs and the loyalty of candlelit shelters,
full of a cabaret melancholy I swallow like red wine.
A history filled with matinée idols rushing to rescue me
from the utter loneliness of my dreams.

Who are you loyal to, Jakob,
who would you say no to, for whose sake?
You have a kindness inside your anger
that makes your violent century bearable
but you are a man like a man I know
and I must ask you this, forgive me Jakob,
who have you destroyed by not looking back?

It is your work to keep walking
sweet-voiced and urgent ahead of your children.
Your house is full of love and its walls are made only of thoughts,
and you will keep leaving to go to work and returning
to build new walls against the winds that follow you

and under the bare sky of the future
I will shelter in my heart
the small nest of history you built for me there.

III

Ox blood poisons the ground with longing

Ox blood poisons the ground with longing
for better times long gone.

Through the suburban streets the lowing of beasts before death
shadows the grass verges and turns the jacarandas red.

Even those who never knew where to pour their libations
understand that there were things they should have asked

of the spirits in another language now lost to everyone
except the oxen walking between cars

to die here,
knowing it is no use.

The words in their blood run away into the tar
as soon as their faithful necks are slashed open.

Visiting home

In a lull,
on a low-news long weekend,
the president goes home to propitiate
(thank, ask, apologise, libate)
his ancestors.

His mother sighs and orders cattle
for the slaughter ceremony,
the villagers and media crews,
and Jik for the blood.

What else to do?
It is, after all, the story of the past.
Times do come when this story is
urgently needed.

So if the president can fit in now
a digitisation of the old home movie,
we should take advantage of the moment.
He's doing it for all of us.

The air will be disturbed
and afterwards will settle,
and whatever was in the air
hoping or watching –

the curious wind,
and the president's mother's memories
as she washes the sheets and hangs them in the sun,
the ones the president slept on as a child.

He can't explain

He can't explain, so he just says
'I'm writing about corruption'
and everyone at the dinner table goes 'ah'.
They're glad, as if now that a poet is taking it on
something might happen.

All their transactions with reality are brittle,
there are broken cells in every contract.
They pass examples down to him
and turn their attention to the visiting oncologist
their host is sponsoring, rising to follow her into the next room
for liqueurs, each with a personal invitation to extend.

He stays at the table,
trying to fold away everything into his pockets.
The tablecloth lifts its wings, it wants to get out
but the heavy plates are holding it down
and the wine stains, and the fruit peels turning soft and brown.

Outside and inside the temple

Where I live the sacrifices happen daily
now, one life costs another.
These are private transactions,
the priests stay clear.

The turnover in deaths and births is very fast.
No one is cutting down the roses, they've grown so big
they completely obscure the windows of the temple.
From inside the sky looks pure red.

Corruption – a lexicon

break
open
expand
bend
twist
change
persuade
invite
teach
help
win
reward
faster
higher
yes

away from towards through around in the dark in the light for one
for all with words with looks with touch with money with favours
helpfully kindly willingly gently secretly once often

use your know-how
take advantage of the situation
think laterally
what this country needs are entrepreneurial skills
cast thy bread upon the waters
love thy neighbour as thyself
never look a gift horse in the mouth
you're worth more than this
it's not what you know it's who you know
blood is thicker than water
a person is a person because of other people

Evolution: details

Note the hand's grasping motion,
the opposing thumb, the free articulation of the joints,
how easily it changes shape
to grip whatever it finds.
Humanity began here
with the power to hold,
to run while holding.

Studies have shown the heart's chambers
expanding each time a chosen object comes
into the line of vision. Certain cell receptors open their mouths,
pores on the skin dilate. The object varies from case to case
but the general phenomenon is identical in all humans
and is commonly referred to as love.

How her mother prepared her

It had a fluffy breast
and wing feathers like sprayed silk
obstinately curved,
the dove her mother put into her hands

that nestled there,
seeming to be real –
the jade magenta bruise
pulsing its throat,

something inside the body
warming it,
something beating
against her fingers like a heart

day after day,
her hands growing
around the growing bird.
Then the next child was born.

Her mother sliced the bird
lengthwise through,
sewed up the raw edges
and gave half back to her.

One full hand felt
the downy bloodwarm whisper of a heart,
the other cold air
scouring its skin.

The half dove kept
its loving eye on her
like a challenge
or a desperate question

so she held on to it
and the empty air
raging and grieving,
year by year learning

to know the scarred
rising and falling ribs
along which half her love
slid like useless foam.

Her mother said,
keep that for yourself,
but she had begun by pouring it all into the dove
and could not stop.

Her fingers try still
to unstitch the scars,
to pour it in that way
so that what's missing will grow back.

Engineers of dreams

The smoky scent of bodies juicing each other
and the slow reach of a tongue
into the folds of warmth –
salt lives here, and the softest skin.

It is always dark
where bodies join so completely,
the sun draws a thundercloud around itself
to hide from this heat.

Where bodies join
and hair tangles thoughtlessly
bellies and thighs rub at the hard muscles
holding back death's great flower

and there is a moment of bursting
that even reading this you imagine
as if you were tasting the salt of that garden,
as if you were there, folded into that story you know well,

now seized and melted down and cast into the words of men
describing how they lit a fire under two people on a spit
and watched them roast and sizzle while they drank their beers
in the quiet veld, while they braaied their lunch and drafted reports.

Now that these men have built a road to this place
I go there night after night, dreaming and waking.

IV

In the cradle of humankind

Geological time locates us
at the crossroads of hominids and democracy,
wiser or younger or older or more harmonised
than the non-miraculous nations of the world.

We used to be teeth like grubby stones
packed solid in warm earth.
Our teeth were enough to tell
the fossilised story of our lives.

Something unearthed us,
broke us open, flung us out
into the big black nowhere of the universe.

Something rearranged the coal dust of our souls
so that we could have the momentary radiance of flowers,
and become rubies more precious than blood.

Every revolution begins in the streets

Gorgeous, gleaming
like plums soaked in brandy
set alight by the last kitchen match

these dreams burn delicious holes in the heart,
blue flames shimmering
hungrily around an empty space,
Audi-shaped.

At last freedom comes.
They rise up from their underground bays.

Parked outside the ghetto house
of the proudest mother in the world
each Audi fills the front yard
almost to bursting.

Roaring off, sucking the air after it.
The vacuum fills with small appliances.
For mother, a special gift:
lipstick, Audi-coloured.

Tannie Lettie plays the guitar

Tannie Lettie plays the guitar,
from above with her index finger,
the way you cut cake.
She says it's because it's strung the Hawaiian way.
We sing hallelujahs; we pray.
Yes, everyone must pray, says Tannie Pike.

Heila asked for time off from Checkers to be here.
We must pray that her husband finds work.
Louise has her retarded child with her –
he bangs his head against the chair non-stop.
Emmenis's mother sits next to her, with grey hair
hanging below her shoulders and a glistening cataract eye –
she keeps pulling flakes of skin off her elbows.
Before she prays, it looks as if she's starting to draw
blood: 'Amen! Lord, God, Djesus, amen amen!'
she shouts. 'Amen, amen,' Tannie Pike calms her down.

I don't know what this is about but it happened,
it's still happening.

Prometheus resigns from the Party

To be ordinary
becomes his desire,
to be camouflaged inside confusion
by the mottled moral complexion of the unstreamlined
unmassaged unenhanced days and nights
surviving one by one fate's endurance tests
without thunderbolts or blazing chariots or a goddess's love,
to be lumpy, muted, slightly ungrammatical,
to backtrack, go off at a tangent, repeat himself,
exaggerate, underestimate, miscalculate,
to wear out his shoes and get lost inside his jacket,
at all costs to avoid transfiguration, to avoid shining.

Only a good man

He walks home through a spring meadow
he doesn't see, drunk, falling against flowers
he has no use for. Paper clips, he thinks,
staples, punched holes. Binding.
Bound copies. Don't lose a single page.

Up to his knees in yellow and purple flowers
on thin stems so elastic his heavy boots just bounce them
down and up again behind him.
The olives on these trees
will take a thousand years to ripen.

Lizards scatter as his shadow grows
but today he means no one any harm.
Envelopes. Bundles. He needed to buy an answer
from a man in an office who never knows his name.
Halfway he knew what it cost

and halfway he just couldn't do that thing.
The searchlight of his child's questions
tracks his silence all night.
He is turning his home into things he can sell
and things that are worthless.

In the morning he starts out again. Behind his boots
the flowers bounce back up, hopeful
as only useless meadow flowers can be.
Lizards spread out on the warm gravel around his door,
shitting tiny seeds as they go.

The personal assistant

Smaller than a paper clip
magnetised
with tips that extend
silently
or in the dark,

inside his master's armour
he runs up and down
working the levers.

He's the one to be careful of,
the one without the speeches,
the one who keeps the borders open between yes and no.

He knows spells that only work
in silence, or in the dark,
for bringing armies to their knees.
Sunlight obeys him, and building plans.

With a signature, a date, a key turned or lost
he conquers countries and your fate before breakfast
and returns them apparently unharmed
to his master for the meeting, the press conference, the handshake.

Redistributing it

Water sloshes over into the new hollows
finding its level again
and the weight of it lies a little differently
over the earth.
Stolen air is swallowed now in different corridors,
the map of suffocation redraws itself.

The dogs track theft's footprints steadfastly
through offices and parliaments.
These cupboards splintered by laws,
these gardens carried away as evidence.
Bring the food trucks and the milk trucks
to this side now.

Mass death has moved in here,
the groaning old woman in the child's house,
and the child at the door looking out
with her wide clean eyes like empty bowls,
and the dogs moving past,
noses to the perfumed road.

Preparing to govern

They can't have water
but they can have
taps.

Inherited
surplus
abandoned
taps

everywhere in every house:
in cupboards
in rows along walls
at every corner of the window
beside each mattress.

Water waits in a raw ditch
at the far end of an endless White Paper

but from the taps come
honey wine oil milk
saved and poured lovingly into pipes
to be caught and saved
as the taps open and close,
open and close for each child, each woman, each man –

days of abundance
at the hand's command.

Oral tradition

He's heard the stories
of a century of slow pain,
slow struggle, slow change
slipping back every day.

The wind blowing down everything built,
the bruised bodies, the jerseys with holes in them.

This boy does skyscraper deals at the speed of sound
and they hold, they seem to hold.
In six months he's accumulated
more than his parents' bosses earned in a lifetime.

Where are the old slow forces
that moved barefoot across stones and years?

This boy's mind seems light and strong
in the way that a plane's wings are strong,
flexible, familiar with moving air,
with the wind's flight paths.

He has such weak legs,
he will never be able to walk away from the crash site.

Shopping

Now this is as good a place as any
and no one has changed
but let's be fair, everyone's found
something inside they'd forgotten
since birth or before
so you can go shopping now for yourself,
you can find bargains in your own head
and sell them right here where the ground burns your feet.

A cellphone is everyone's doorway.
You can send yourself everywhere you can't go
and have conversations instead of listening to yourself.
Who do you want to be? Try this number.

There are ring tones on offer to express your most unique dreams.
You should remember to check the rear view mirror
but apart from that do anything you can think of,
you'll discover so many soulmates you never imagined
all tripping over the same obstacles
in their hurry to meet you.

And the obstacles? They have cellphones too.
Talk to them. Ask them what they cost.

Stop child abuse

The cheapness of the songs they teach this child
is where it starts. They make her clap her hands,
they make her sing 'My bodee is my bodee',
they make her smile at the TV cameras like a rescued seal.

The little girl is sewn onto the letterheads and T-shirts
of the Ministry of Health, the Ministry of Welfare and the
                                        Ministry of Education.
Tonight her father and her uncle and her teacher will rip her off
                                        the T-shirts,
push her head into the cushion and rape her.

Tomorrow the Ministry of Police will show the world the teddy bear
they want the child to hold while they take her broken statement.
She is fully integrated into the fabric of her society
and she sings its meretricious songs as if they were magic spells.

At night in the dark she whispers the words over and over to her father
                                        and her uncle and her teacher
and they force themselves between her lips to stop her singing.

Wind parted the buildings

Wind parted the buildings.
Men and women were exposed
each on a pavement alone,
playing hopscotch, avoiding the cracks
to stay close to luck.

There was a plane flying overhead.
It came down low, circling slowly.
Faces peered from cabin windows,
video cameras angled to capture the streets.

Leaves and cigarette butts blew through.
Ladders dangled from high windows.
Luck was at the bus station, reading the timetable
with an off-peak ticket in her hand
valid only for certain routes.

Three-stringed necklace

Threaded on a fine string
all the men raping all the women
and the swift bright virus of hell spiralling through them.

Threaded on a fine string
the crisis of overproduction and the hunger of every person
and the tiny beads of capitalism keeping them from touching.

Threaded on a fine string
the children's memories of the ones they trusted
and their blood rusting the knots.

Clasped around the world's unsteady throat
the necklace catches the sun
and lets it fall, lets it fall.

So very sick

So very sick,
clearly dying,
the Minister of Defence was still organising
ways to increase his wealth.

And his son already dead.
And his golden reputation already forged
now melting in the furnace
of his deals. Accountants, brokers, lawyers
heating the fire for him, carrying him
sick and bloated into his own meltdown,
the unhappy eyes, the small mouth.

Hero amputating his own feet,
making himself new ones of clay,
painting them gold, the cheapest kind of paint.

Triptych

Can you be better than this?
A bird has been sitting outside your window
for years with this question clutched in its throat.
Can you? Can you?

You look up all the time to see if it's there,
which is your answer.

*

Sometimes the water washes the seabed completely clean.
In its colourless cradle
crushed shells, sea moss and sleeping fish rock,
seeming freshly created.

Beyond the shallow pools the sea returns
to its blackness, its unreachable pearls.

*

On the darkest wall of the room an etched crow hangs
nailed to a table, black-eyed, dead.
The glass covering it has captured a mass of green leaves
outside the window opposite, sunlit and moving.

The leaves completely hide the crow,
as if it had broken a hole in the wall
and planted a tree there
and flown away from the tree.

Somewhere nearby you can hear weeping,
perhaps because of you.

Flakes of the light falling

plague poem

approximately and here also
one in four vanishing
even as we speak –

lightly and without technique they are dying
slowly and beyond the duration of love

good citizens of a good country, dying modestly
embrace of the infected is a national project
rejection the prerogative of the intimate circle

metaphors of love crack open,
out of their varnished shells
people emerge, dying

howling is not possible where children sleep
and their mothers, dying blossoms of blue light
inside the cloudbursts of men's love

very close to the ground children and their mothers
and then also their fathers die here
in the way of poor people, struggling
for small dignities and the simplest food
astonished softly over and over
I touch my lips to each death

approximately and here also
one in four vanishing –

how many little pallbearers for one coffin?
to wrap your father in a sheet takes days and days
tangling yourself in the web of bones
who will bury him if you don't?

you saw helplessly at the tree

all night my little clock makes a vastly solemn noise
like a child treading the long dark passage
in her grandfather's shoes

among blades of grass, against crumbled walls
let cows offer their udders to the babies
lying upturned, helpless as beetles

metaphors of love crack open

suddenly one day you will hear
how silently the black sky blazes
how wildly the empty street is searching
for a footstep

we are ending, we are ending
flakes of the light falling away

V

Book

page 1

Here you are. Will you go further?

page 2

A small rabbit sits in the middle of a road.

What do you think of when you read this?

Perhaps the flat stretch between Laingsburg and Beaufort West,
the road works, the ostriches that come over the hill
to stare at the waiting cars.

Perhaps night, the rabbit's eyes shining.

Perhaps what you did in a car once on that road, also at night,
with a wonderful man, driving at very high speed.

Think of the little rabbit on the white line.
Cars are thundering by.

page 3

It's early morning, whisperstill.
Walking in the veld
a man was touched on one side
by the palest light.

Look back.
Can you still see the road?

page 4

Pushed into a clump of thorn bushes
a hut clutches at the spines of shade.
No clues about the owner, though this is private land.
There's one like it on every page
without windows, a doorway with no door.

If you wait here someone might come.
The hut looks abandoned
but there's a canvas bag against one wall.
You could wait, or move on.
That might be breath you hear, or the sound of footsteps.

page 5

Standing near a barbed wire fence
why do you have the feeling
something bad happened here
once or many times?

You know more about this place than you can explain.

page 6

What are you thinking of?
When you look at this hill
knowing which country you're in,
what images spread themselves on the ground
among the splintered pink stones scattered everywhere,
softening the light?

page 7

This is a very barren place.
Dreaming doesn't make it better.

You could watch a *film noir* on television.
When it was over your room would feel brighter, gentler –
a nest of yellow cushions.

Out here the sounds and textures challenge your skin
to grow scales, or feathers. Learn to caw, to hiss, to buzz
between the mimosa petals spattered with your blood.

But you can walk here. Your boots won't go through the page.

page 8

Is the rabbit still there?
Is it alive?

You can't sit in the hut forever.

To find out would mean going back.

page 9

So, you landed in a rabbit's story
on a national road
in a wide country.

Not even water was provided.

Or stories about lives
a little like yours.
Someone whose heart was bruised
like yours by someone
like someone you love.
Not a rabbit, unless
it has a soul like yours,
unless it is a symbol.
Are you perhaps a symbol for the rabbit?

page 10

A road and a stretch of veld
unspooled
across a blank page.

Cars and plants in a landscape.

If the rabbit is still there
it is by now flecked flesh and blood
staining the paper.

Were you there?
Did you come back?

VI

It seems that if you write

It seems that if you write
of a place outside your heart
it is a country.
People look for a name
and stamp it on your tongue. A crest.

Your words get stuck in the furrows and ridges
like shreds of meat.
Your mouth starts to stink like a hyena's lair.
The place you were going to with your words
has ended here.
It will be found in the teeth of fossils
dug out three thousand years hence
and used to name the ones who ate you.

You were writing of a place you hadn't got to yet.
Like the honeysuckle's breath on the night air,
its perfume vanished as you got close.

This other place

The place of engraved pain and ecstasy,
cave crowded with demons and gods
casting spells into which we invite strangers and detain them,
hollow ourselves out to contain them.

The place where it is permitted to talk of love.

*

Cupboard doors broken open
leaning against their hinges,
heads dangling from ropes,
skin stretched between tree trunks.

Turn this way, turn that,
what's hidden there waits for you.

Don't touch the teardrops on the bronze fennel fronds
brushing your legs – each is a spell,
a kiss's shroud, a ghost's shell,
don't touch, don't touch.

In doorways

In doorways
we hold on to each other

stay here
take me with you

look, I am this red silk heart unfolding
keep unfolding me, there's more

stay here
take me with you

we go out alone
air separating all our surfaces

but there you are, in the sky above my road
your face pressed against a small window, waving to me

relative to you I am everywhere
and you, you are my longest journey

reaching home you'll find yourself already here
robed in red silk: come back, bring me back

Between them

Between them they create a third body
which is themselves in love: a silhouette
of an embrace, and each returns there
more often or less often as things grow
between them.

Something tears,
there are raw fibres on both sides
clutching at air.

Breath by breath it tears a little further,
they hear it in the night, bones breaking inside a heart,
a matchstick house cracking.

In my sleep

In my sleep I wake
trying to hold on to you
in this room full of dark, hot air
and your sleeping body drifting
in some secret place
beside me, far away.

Watching you translate yourself into your next embrace
I know that what I hold is just that old discursive figure
'the lover in his lover's arms',
a construct of a dream.

The hurting pillow

The hurting pillow is the one that bears the dreams all night
holding my neck twisted against air
like a bird half-strangled by winds turning its throat
away from its wings.

From what cells in my body come these stories
of flies encrusted with silver-crumbed maggots?
From what chemistry the precise amount of R81,
my worth for an evening's work
serving the man and the woman I know but never name?

And the man lies beside me while I twist on the pillow
and in the morning I serve him for free
and weep into his soft neck,
the tender place where I sleep easily.

Cured

Is there a moment
when you feel better,
cured?

Glass glued together
still edges carefully
along its shatter lines.

The glue veins, thicker than the rest,
stride matron-like across
the fragile sunlight of the skin.

Love and loneliness and longing
sparkle like bad clusters
inside the alienated lightness of you.

What was there before?
It's gone.
Try not to tear your shadow open, looking for it.

VII

Walking songs for Africans abroad

A travelling game

There's a game we play when we travel abroad.
Looking up from a drink in a bar, a museum queue, a souvenir counter
we ask, where are the Africans?

We ask, where are the Africans?
And we answer each other in different ways
depending on the mood we're in.
It's a way to pass through the hours of estrangement,
a way to walk through the galleries of strange looks from strangers.

The game ends when one of us says,
that's a non-question.

Or when we realise there are non-African friends among us
looking hurt, or starting to apologise for something.
We change the subject then. It's seldom worth the effort
of trying to explain this isn't about them.

One of us alone may ask the question silently
stepping out into the morning of a foreign city,
like a ghost setting out to haunt an unfamiliar house.
It's a way of comforting ourselves, recalling that there must be
other ghosts like us, and that we all haunt houses where we've never lived.

At Lago di Garda they have other problems

Lago di Garda is a beautiful place, laced with settings
                              for Goethe's dreams of the south.
Walking along the narrow road between Sompriezzo and Pieve
you understand at last the things in your childhood anthologies:
cowbells, hazelnut trees, Jews hidden in caves and barns, bramble berries.

Around the lake itself cypresses preen, lemon groves pretend
                              an ancient elegance
and the *gelati* are pistachio, vanilla, cherry and lime just as they should be.
I looked around unrestfully, not knowing why.

The light was chiffon everywhere, a kind of silence
filtering the chatter of the promenade away from anything true.

I thought I saw a dark shape walking up a side street
and my skin changed as if someone familiar had touched me.
But it was gone, or never there; only the cool palazzo walls stared past me.
I knew I must be the only person in this whole town who could
                                                                                    even imagine
what my real world is like, so much light and earth, so much
                                                                                    sleeping and growing.

But later I watched the tired owner of the *gelateria* locking his doors
and realised he'd probably been trying to speak German all day to
                                                                                    Bavarian tourists.
Nobody really cares what anyone else's world is like, unless
                                                                                    they're writing a PhD.
It's not a crime against humanity.

Thesaurus entries for 'Africans Abroad'

> in transit
> transitory
> transitional
> transient

The sociological fraud

If you ask the wrong question, you get the wrong answer.
An African taught me that.

I ask them anyway, when I get lonely.
The answers astonish each time, like onions.

For example:
Why is the first human you see at any airport
a black man handling luggage?

Why do American novelists still divide their characters
into 'characters' and 'black characters'?

Why are there no African skinheads or *au pairs*?

At conferences we learn so much

To stand inside your theories, unuttered,
produces a dizziness. Caught between the lushness of my world
and its absence here. Do you think your ruling class's surplus capital
came from a hole in the ground in Greenland?

Talking and talking you talk, my dedicated friends,
and all that you know teeters on a point of blindness
your toes fail to sense, clutching the soles of your feet,
thinking they are the whole earth's curve supporting you.

Local rabbits in smart jeans, you're thermally well-protected and
                                        anxious for change,
just checking the time on your perfect watches.
Do you ever look at your backs in the mirror?
From my country we see them all the time,
the raw edges, the sand trickling out of the seams,
                                        the drought-stricken heels.
Millions of tiny seamstresses still working on you.

You welcome us, we are your cautionary tales, your myths,
                                        your keynote speakers,
the parts of you that walked across the mined desert to get here.
You wish you could have a miracle like ours,
a sort of atom bomb of festivity to clear the past out of the way.

The puzzled looks on our faces you take for a problem of language,
and devote yourselves to whispering translations of the speeches in our ears.
You're right, in a sense; we don't have a language for saying
where do your questions come from?

Hanging around in corners like one of Jane Austen's minor girls,
I'm trying to tuck my continent in behind me
so no one trips on it. But it's so damned big.
I should never have tried to bring it with me.

'Wear ethnic dress,' they ask all delegates.
As if history were a diorama in a department store window
and not the bright patterns of blood on all our bedroom floors.
Their ethnic dress is black leather with a touch of something striped.
Nepalese, Guatemalan.
Very cool.

Born travellers

We're born travellers. We compose walking songs, songs of
building the boss's roads, songs of the long train journey to the
mines, songs of our lovers abandoning us for city women, songs of
living in hostels without our children, of standing at passport
offices, of being in exile, of tracking a cow or a lion or a USAID
management studies programme. We invented a piano the size of
our hearts to play as we walk.

We've been travelling forever. There's a map that shows how
Africans spread across the world to populate it; the cartographers
called it 'Africans: the first colonisers'. Some of us have objected to
being called that. We're more comfortable with the modest role of
loving our birthplace and wanting it back. But we keep on
travelling, in the holds of ships and down mine shafts, with crates
of goods to sell and dossiers of crimes to recount. We have so
much left to give, so many blood diamonds and bleached bones, so
many muted languages and ecstatic dances. Over and over again
we re-populate the world with our evolving pain and curiosity,
replenishing each present moment with the DNA of history.

'At the round earth's imagined corners'

After another one of those trips
someone sees his colleague at the airport queuing for the pay phone
and says, 'ET phone home …'
and she says, 'This *is* home, aren't we the world's brothers and sisters?'
and he says, 'Tell that to the passport officers'
and they laugh, and inside they each feel a little sick,
and on the plane each one wakes at some point during the flight
to jot down a few words in a diary, notes for a song or a poem.

Everywhere in the Duomo

Confused European peasants looking in wonder
at a man in authority and a woman standing among them
wrapped in mystery – painting after painting
records life as it was so long ago.

The awed angle of the back repeated body by body,
the billowing centrality of the prince's red cloak,
the play of halo light over modest faces
and always a bird or a dog excluded from everyone's gaze

continuing to live unnoticed.
We wander through like particles in another dimension.
There are no painters who can capture us in a stillness like this.
Looking up, heads craned, eyes struggling to penetrate the dark

we get tired and move on. Moving on is our signature gesture,
unpaintable, and not mysterious.

Globalisation 1

From a distance
everyone looks human.

Even the gun-toting weebly-wobbly doll
in his tight shoes, with his handlers.

Even the dark-eyed dragon watching
all kinds of prophetic chickens come home to roost in his beard.

Even the bundle of melted flesh
lying at an angle to its wailing father.

From a distance you think –
there's someone I know, I'll wave, I'll invite him in for coffee.

Globalisation 2

Loudly you fall over me like bricks
with your song of growth
through loans through contracts through programmes
poured down the boreholes of conditionalities
your system digs through this continent.
In the earthquake of your voice I crack and collapse
and all that protects me now is this whispered No,
this small air pocket I live in.

Letters to the president

1

Dear Mr President,
If I could just –
If you could –

I need to trust you.

2

It can only work
if I believe
you're like me.

It can only work
if you rescue the people
I'd rescue
if I had your power.

3

You're doing such terrible things in my name.
Mutely I sit here
choking on my humanity.

4

Because I'm not Mandelstam or Hikmet,
because my words can do you no harm and save no one from you,
because you step over me daily without even deliberate mercy,
because you expect me to eat blindfolded,

I stand outside your door offering up my small amount of breath
to curse you when there is sweet air to swallow
and for that I curse you too.

Why could you not be
someone I could love?

Bat in my hair, steering me.

Dear Mr President –
Dear President –
Dear person dragging the whole country behind you
like a plough across the brutal field of your imagination –
Dear person dragging the brutal plough of your imagination
across the hopeful field of this country –

The word 'dear' means beloved, or precious, cherished.
It implies affection.
It can also mean that a thing is high-priced
relative to its real value.
Its origin is in the Old English word *dēor*
which meant brave, or severe,
and it came to be used for something that was hard, grievous.
Mr President, how are you dear to us,
whose dreams are haunted by your nightly pacing?

Distantly heard signals

'Left wing coup in Ecuador. 22 January 2000.'
Can there be any doubt that it will fail?
Already they must be starting the helicopters in Washington.
The bankers will be on the phone.
Tomorrow it'll all be over.

But not.
Each uprising a voice from deep space,
the prime numbers of humanity beamed in our direction
from the ones who lived it fully, briefly
in a distant universe.

Their signal was switched on there
and it keeps travelling.

Aching

If I could just
catch the man falling
there, so high, so tiny

if I could just
push my hand through the screen
into the burning city

I'd be bleeding, he'd be screaming,
the terror would be real
inside, here

there's smoke and ash pushing against the glass
trying to reach me –

Or if I come outside,
lie down in the wet grass until my skin shivers,
smell the green night rubbing my cheeks

if in the sky over Refrontolo
a satellite can find me, take my picture,
show it to the people in New York

who'll lean towards their screens fascinated, aching
through this distance –

*

In Frankfurt I stand one arm's length
from a woman on display
and in my chest a burning grows
that I mistake for sadness and then recognise as shame.

No one should come this close
even to the bronze and oil paint simulacrum of a moment
of such detailed inwardness. Every fold and freckle of her sagging face
stands still for me to catalogue. This pain cracking my heart open

is the artist's trick. He's pushed me through the screen.
The woman's eyes refuse mine, her lips stay closed.
The words that name me come out of my own mouth:
Housebreaker. Violator. Thief.

*

Don't stare, it's rude.
And empathy is rape.
And kindness is, like hunger, loss of self.

What is the right distance for touching?

They say if you want a dog to come to you
stand still, don't run towards it, calling.

And when it comes?

Collioure, September 2001

A warm afternoon, overcast sky, calm sea.
Across the bay four squads of young recruits
row back and forth, timing their strokes.

The water's lapping stillness seeps through café conversations
about fauvists, espadrilles, anchovy fleets.
Someone calls out, 'Don't they know there's no coastline in Afghanistan?'
Laughter shudders across the tables like an eel.

Fanned out around the harbour
the houses catch light in their quiet façades.
Artists have made a wild palette out of these sunburnt sorbets,
extracting from them something more than tranquillity
which now the children copy, cross-legged on the salty cobblestones,
in the bold strokes their teacher shows them,
then slither down the slipway
to perch on the crumbling boats for photos, buy ice creams
and lure each other backwards into poodle droppings.

Here as everywhere in this age of atonement tourism,
the monument to transported Jews.
On the path between the fortress and the church
a fresh steel sail and mast
blindingly bright over the stone that names just thirteen,
the ones allowed to leave six hundred years ago.

Tourists emerging from the castle stop at the bridge over the little moat
to watch the teenage soldiers shake their hair dry,
deflate their war craft, load them on their backs
and wait for the next order from their sergeant.

He's out on the breakwater gazing at something, smoking.
His brother has set up an easel on the beach facing the newsagent's stall.
They both were born in these hills and seldom talk,
but it can happen that they find themselves on the same stretch
                                        of coast at the same time,
trying to visualise what the light will do, and the water.

Soft

Soft on a summer bed in the Languedoc
a man in an Afghan prison sits with me
watching his brother walking through snowdrifts
to a village much like this one
(boucherie, tabac, boulangerie, broken shutters)
where a month's supply of bullets lies secured
in a box beneath his mother's wedding carpet.

Turning the pages of Bruce Chatwin's life
I feel the ashy bodies shift and stutter downward
through steel sticks broken on New York's southern streets.
Peruvian feathers hang in coloured blocks
across the whiteness of a wall in England,
the man in the snow takes another step forward,
under a sky-blue burqa a woman writes to the man in prison
without pen or paper.

Together we turn the pages, always together now.
Lavender. Ash. Snow on a black beard.

Marseillette – Kabul – New York, September 2001

Apprehension, north

four firs at dusk come to this garden
watching

at treetop height I wait behind glass

four fierce messengers from a winter king
watching

this yellow room pretends sunlight for me

four tower guards inside a green-thatched castle
watching

a spider tells my movements in silk

four curious royal children behind green curtains
watching

fireflies come close to photograph me

four hooded warlocks summoned to wake the forest
watching

my hands behind the glass grow cold
the spell takes hold

A certain history

Dust is shy,
like fallen hair.

Together they go
to the shelter of corners,

gathering in small furry stillnesses
like servants of the deceased at a funeral,

or drift up a lamp stand,
across the top of an armchair,

waiting to be removed.
In the empty late afternoon sunlight

they float unobserved, gold shimmering mosaics inlaid in air
as if by artists of rare skill, celebrating a certain history.

Wednesday morning in the Café Caprice

There's a sledgehammer going steadily
in the upper left corner of the roof.

A roar of steam from the cappuccino jet.

A rotary machine drying itself
or the air or something else helpless and silent.

Someone knocking espresso bricks out of their mould
against the side of a bin, metal on metal.

Dean Martin crooning his love
to a thousand violins.

The garbage van compacting the street's refuse
in four dimensions of decibels.

Teaspoons clattering onto saucers.

A fly coughing and coughing on my arm.

Across the road the sea in its own silent movie
throwing up waves, catching them in its blue arms.

He is often mentioned in books

Who is Li Po,
and why was he always drunk?

I know a man like that,
is he also Li Po?

I would like to be that one,
the one you think of when you say the word 'happiness',

or try to tell how it is to fall down
with your own exhaustion, shouting at fate.

Everyone I know is only a little bit of himself
and then back, back into the office and the bedroom.

Though there are the ones who phone late at night,
who send their works unfinished, who make you drive for four hours –

they are all Li Po's brothers and sisters
but without the sweetness of his smile.

Reaching Siran

Time travellers with maps at the wrong scale
we look around this dusty site
confused at eye level, dissatisfied.

The church is shut. Nailed to the stone
photocopied notices tangle with the wind
trying to attract our attention. What's that smell?

Crushed underfoot tough spearmint twigs release their scent a little at a time,
green amphorae of lemon thyme rub oil against our legs,
the lavender fans sweep our bending cheeks.

Vines hold the hill in all directions. Their heavy grapes are sweet
                                                    with centuries of heat.
The juice soaks through our lips, our fingers scrabble stickily at the well
but the clear black water's eye laughs up at us from too far down.

Translation rights

The contract's useless.
You'll never know what happened to your work.
Cheques, if they arrive, will be like carrier pigeons
with their tongues cut out
to prevent you learning where they come from.

Perhaps in Japan the poems are held
between a peach blossom bough and a band of red silk
in someone's private shrine,
becoming paler and more honest.

Or in a green-spiked heat haze children are skipping
to memorise the lines, and they become
parrot-bright between shacks.

Or they have died into library binding.

Your life. Translated into hostages and brides and lanterns,
dark skies and bright skies passing through the calendar.

No wonder you wake so often lost, and full of wonder.

Ends that hang over the lake

The man who can't go back to Poland.
The man who won't go back to England until he's dead.
The woman who made a house out of the children's secrets,
paper walls that dissolved in winter.

The sound at night of a roof tile
falling down a hill of air, soft splash
into water in a dream.

The moon passing, pausing, passing.

Morning cows walk firmly
toward the inland meadows.
Vines wrap their arms around the impetuous rose.

The man who won't go back to Poland.
The man who can't go back to England until he's dead.
The woman, wife of a lost translator,
who throws her house stone by stone into the lake.

Sompriezzo, September 2001
for Anne and Hans

The work the poets do

When the terrible moment is over
what's left are splinters of rubies
and the poets collecting them
    'Black milk of daybreak we drink it at evening'

When the tongues have shrivelled
what's left are threads of the uniforms caught on barbed wire
and the poets collecting them
    'we drink it at midday and morning we drink it at night'

When the eyelashes have flown away
what's left are the shrapnel twigs
and the poets collecting them
    'we drink and we drink'

Battle ground sweepers
collecting the claws the gold teeth the faint echoes
the shreds of old light the burnt flowers the torn books
the bones and the ghosts in their chests,
and singing
        and singing all night
        like children whose parents haven't come home

The canary's songbook

The incredibly cheerful canary
hasn't stopped singing all morning
out of her cage at last, down here
among the dark wetly alluring rocks
in the long mysteriously endless tunnel.

She's free and she sings
every song she remembers
and others she's never heard before
and she takes no notice of the people passing
who say 'oh no, not another canary metaphor',
she's having such a good time,
she's having the time of her life.

Her songbook is as old as the hills
and as familiar as birds chattering and footsteps marching past.
She's learning it page by page,
amazed that her voice knows the way.

She could have been a rosebush facing a row of vines,
dying ahead of them in a cloud of eager fungus
to save their precious skins

but she'd rather be down here among the rocks
that flash their gold smiles in the pool of darkness
she stares into, thinking she sees a beautiful canary there.

You have to imagine her in the tunnel singing
and the wet rocks shining
and the men retreating to safety.